RADI

ISLAM

HOW WOULD
JESUS RESPOND?

GARY MILLER

ISBN: 978-1-943929-33-7

All Scripture quotations taken from the New King James
Version (NKJV).

Illustrations: Gavin Miles

Cover graphics: © Shutterstock.com

Second printing: January 2017

Published by:
TGS International
P.O. Box 355, Berlin, Ohio 44610 USA
Phone: 330-893-4828
Fax: 330-893-2305
www.tgsinternational.com

TGS001389

Table of Contents

Radical Islam

The Internet is full of violence, but even hardened news junkies were unprepared for such a barbaric sight. The video immediately went viral as viewers around the globe tried to wrap their minds around the horrific scene.

It was August 19, 2014, and a stunned world watched in astonishment.

"This is James Wright Foley, an American citizen of your country," said a voice with a thick accent. "As a government, you have been at the forefront of the aggression towards the Islamic State."

Foley, a forty-year-old journalist from Rochester, New Hampshire, is on his knees with a wide expanse of desert behind him. A masked Islamic militant dressed in black stands at his side, brandishing a long knife.

"You have plotted against us and have gone far out of your way to find reasons to interfere in our affairs. Today, your military air force is attacking us daily in Iraq. Your strikes have caused casualties among Muslims."

The clip continues with James Foley asking President Obama to stop the bombing of innocent people in Islamic countries. He reads a message, presumably carefully scripted by his captors, stating that his "real killer" is America.

"I wish I had more time. I wish I could have the hope for freedom to see my family once again,"[1] he says in a monotone, the camera recording the chilling scene.

The man dressed in black then warns America that more people will die just like this if the bombing doesn't stop. Casually he takes his knife, firmly grasps James Foley's chin, and begins sawing off his head. The screen goes black for a moment; then the final scene shows Foley's blood-soaked body lying on the sand, his decapitated head on his chest facing the camera.

The video raced around the world as newscasters picked up the story, discussing the ramifications of this horrendous act. Experts were called in and questioned. Why would someone do this? What kind of people could kill in such a cold-hearted way?

And then, just two weeks later, another chilling video. This time it was American journalist Steven Sotloff and the same masked killer. "I'm back, Obama, and I'm back because of your arrogant foreign policy towards the Islamic State."[2]

Again the masked executioner warns President Obama to stop bombing the Islamic State, and again he decapitates his victim. Once more the final scene is the victim's body lying on the sand with his severed head resting on his body.

The immediate outcry against these deplorable acts was overwhelming. News anchors condemned the appalling actions, the public called for retaliation, and politicians took to the airwaves, crying out for revenge. Some called for carpet bombing—just killing anything that moved. Others applied pressure on the government to find the black-hooded Mohammed Emwazi, better known as "Jihadi John," and hold him accountable for his actions.

American Islamic Exposure

Increasingly Westerners are surrounded by people trying to faithfully follow their prophet, Muhammad. Many Americans are asking questions and making strong, polarizing statements. Some declare that all Muslims are the same. They say that the Quran teaches warfare, Islam is a religion of violence, and all Muslims should be viewed as potential threats. They say the religion was built and spread with violence, and radicals are simply taking the Quran to its logical conclusion.

Other Americans disagree. They know Muslims who are friendly, law-abiding citizens. They know them as co-workers or neighbors, hospitable and enjoyable to interact with socially. Consequently, it is easy for this group to distinguish between peaceful Muslims and radical extremist groups. They tend to think of Muslims as nonviolent and are disappointed when people connect the Islamic faith to violence. They know that many Muslims abhor bloodshed and denounce the actions of the radical extremists.

The Unseen Enemy

In addition to those engaging in war in places like

Iraq and Syria, there is another group even more alarming to the West. These would-be jihadists share the goals of radical Muslims in the East, but they dream of conducting jihad in their own Western communities. They live right in the middle of American or European cities, going to work each day, but secretly they desire to launch their own surprise attacks.

Americans listen to newscasters describe Islamic terrorist attacks in the United States, like the 2015 San Bernardino shooting, and they are alarmed. Maybe these attacks are not just isolated events carried out by a few disgruntled people, but are part of a larger organized global effort. A poll taken in 2014 showed that 70 percent of Americans believe ISIS[a] is already in the United States and has the resources to launch a major attack within the country.[3] These Americans are fearful that the wide-scale violence occurring in other countries will soon erupt here, and when they see a Muslim on the street, they feel uneasy.

---

[a] ISIS is an acronym for Islamic State in Iraq and al-Sham or (Islamic State in Iraq and Syria). It is a Sunni Muslim organization whose aim is to restore an Islamic caliphate in the geographical area of Syria, Israel, Lebanon, Jordan, and Southeastern Turkey, and ultimately appears to have its sight on global domination.

Perhaps Americans do have reason for trepidation. Most likely they have people in their own backyards who secretly desire to bring the fight against the West to American soil. The alarming news articles give evidence that this is true. Some of these infiltrators are disgruntled, unfulfilled, and angry at the imbalance of global power and resources. Others are angry at the moral impact the West—primarily America—is having on their home countries and communities. To better understand why many radical Muslims carry such animosity toward America, let's follow the life of a typical young man growing up in Iraq.

CHAPTER TWO

Understanding
the Animosity

The open desert stretched out on each side of the dusty road as Bashir walked back toward his village, perplexed and deep in thought. Kicking at one of the larger stones along the road, the young man seemed oblivious to the honking buses, shouts of playing children, and trucks revving their engines in the rush to get home before dark. In fact, Bashir was almost halfway to his village before he even realized that the Iraqi sky was darkening and a dust storm was approaching.

Reaching down, he picked up a stone and tossed it from hand to hand as he reflected on his life. He had been born into a good Muslim family, and his role models had been faithful followers of the prophet Muhammad. From his earliest days, he had observed these men in his community, and he knew firsthand their deep desire to please Allah. Daily he saw them faithfully set aside the pressing duties of their occupations to pray. As long as he could remember, he had been wakened by the call to prayer. Beginning the day with prayer was as natural as breathing.

First Impressions

As a young lad of six, Bashir had been enrolled in the local madrasa. There he had studied math, science, and reading. He also had memorized large portions of the Quran, learned the basics of Islam, and heard about the prophet Muhammad and his vision from the angel Gabriel in A.D. 610. Now as he walked home, Bashir remembered his history lessons and pondered how they might pertain to today's debate and the choice he must make.

At the madrasa, his teachers had taught him that the religious world of Muhammad's day was corrupt and Allah had commanded the prophet to bring the people back to the true faith. The Islamic faith had quickly spread across the known world. Shortly after Muhammad's death, Muslim armies had miraculously captured all the major urban areas of early Christianity, beginning with Jerusalem in A.D. 636.

Bashir's class had sat spellbound as the teacher recounted those glorious years when Muslims had ruled the world. His heart had thrilled with anticipation as the teacher promised, "Someday Allah will again be worshiped around the world. Someday men will obey him in every country. And it might be soon!" Bashir smiled as he thought back to his childish optimism. It had all seemed so simple then.

Bashir and his friends had also faithfully attended the mosque each week, where their fiery imam would remind them how followers of Jesus had distorted history. Although the prophet Jesus had been sinless, the imam acknowledged, He hadn't actually been crucified. Allah would never have allowed this to happen to one of his prophets! Instead, Jesus had gone back to heaven after being rejected by the Jews he had come to help. The imam explained how Jesus had prophesied that the prophet Muhammad was still to come, saying, "Nevertheless I tell you the truth. It is to your advantage that I go away; for if I do not go away, the Helper will not come to you; but if I depart, I will send Him to you."[a]

Oblivious to the coming storm, Bashir stopped along the road for a moment and thought back to the

---

[a] John 16:7

passion in his imam's voice as he had explained how Muhammad had been this promised helper. What a tremendous fulfillment of prophecy! There had never been a doubt in Bashir's young mind: Jesus was a true Muslim sent by Allah, and Muhammad had come to bring a later and more complete revelation.

The Infidels

Hunching his shoulders against the rising wind, Bashir walked on, his face clouding as he remembered how the imam and his teacher had spoken with disgust about the people called Christians. These infidels polluted Allah's teachings.

"These Christians from America are spreading false teachings, and we must do something to stop them! Their women degrade themselves on public television, dressing immodestly and behaving shamefully! They are a violent and depraved people. Look at any American television program and you will see brazen debauchery!" Bashir could still see his teacher pacing before the class as he explained how this Christian nation, America, spread violence and wickedness all around the world. Halting midstep, he had whirled about, his intense gaze piercing Bashir's soul.

"Not content to promote violence at home, they bring their bombs, destruction, and evil ways to our country! We could be living in peace, but they are killing us and destroying our cities simply because they want our oil!

"Allah must be our only focus! All things are controlled by him, he decides our path, and he is the wellspring of success and prosperity." Pointing to the west, he continued, "But in America, the people mock Allah! They think they can create their own destiny through personal independence. This is a terrible affront to the power of Allah!" Though he was only ten years old at the time, Bashir could clearly remember how his teacher had predicted the spiritual degeneration that would follow if they allowed themselves to be influenced by this dangerous Western culture.

He stopped, gazing into the distance. "Always remember: while we must work hard, our fate and fortune are in the hands of Allah. To believe as the Americans do is blasphemous! They are trying to destroy our culture, our religion, our way of life!"

That was ten years ago, yet to Bashir it seemed like yesterday. That same year his father had left to join the Iraqi resistance, and they had never heard from him again. The years since had brought economic instability, frustration among his peers, and continual political upheaval.

Bashir's brow furrowed as he thought of how his family had struggled to survive without his father and of the many innocent lives lost in the civil war since the American invasion. His teacher's warning that Western influence from Christian nations like America would destroy his country's moral values had proven true. Iraqis who returned after spending time in America or Europe had different standards. They were more independent and showed less respect for the elderly and local religious authorities.

The young women tended to dress immodestly and sneer at those upholding conservative values.

The Answer

As Bashir neared his home, his thoughts turned to that day's discussion in the neighboring village. Several of the young men had met near the center of town, and the debate had become quite lively.

"We are letting these Westerners destroy our culture! The only way to stop them is to join forces with other faithful believers. ISIS needs our help! Are we going to just sit by and let unbelievers rule?"

Some were not so sure. Was more bloodshed really the answer? Bashir had been shocked when one of his close friends suddenly stood and exclaimed, "I believe this is a call from Allah! The world would be better if everyone followed the true and pure Islamic faith. If we allow Western influence to change our culture, what kind of country will our children live in?"

Others agreed, and another of Bashir's friends denounced the evil in the West.

"Over half of Christian marriages end in divorce. Their women have lost their dignity! Unlike our wives, they ignore their role as mothers, leave their children, and work away from home. What is more, they dress and live like harlots!"

Another added, "American Christianity is the chief exporter of immorality, and if we don't fight back, our own children will succumb!"

"At least ISIS will provide food and some income if I join," grumbled another young man who had been trying unsuccessfully to find work. "I am tired of being unemployed."

The dust storm began to blow into the village as Bashir entered his home, the day's conversation continuing to replay in his mind. Several of his friends seemed determined to join the fight and were excited about the possibilities of establishing an Islamic caliphate. They saw ISIS as the answer to their problems and wanted Bashir to join them.

Bashir sat down and stared out the window at the swirling cloud of sand. He longed for peace, yet peace seemed so far away. His father was gone, and last week two of his cousins had been killed in another American airstrike. The glorious Islamic State his teacher used to describe seemed further away than ever. Should he just stay home and let his friends attack the enemy? Should he let others go and die gloriously as martyrs for the cause? Or might joining ISIS be Allah's will for him?

CHAPTER THREE

Christianity from an Eastern Perspective

Living in the Western world, we rarely hear other perspectives. We listen to the news, read our newspapers, and assume our worldview is correct. We seldom have the opportunity to look at our world through the eyes of someone like Bashir. We grow up learning that America is the world superpower that rescues the underdog, feeds the hungry, and liberates people from ruthless dictators.

We forget that many who grow up in Muslim-majority countries see America as having evil intent and a negative impact on the world. And since many consider America a Christian nation, the East sees Christianity as directly responsible for the social corruption they observe.

Whether or not this perception is correct, one

thing is clear. If we are going to comprehend what drives Muslim radicals, we must understand what they believe about Christianity and its effect on the world. We must consider Christianity from an Eastern perspective.

Christians: Promoters of Self-Centeredness

Most people in the Eastern Hemisphere have a deep sense of commitment to community. In contrast, America is known for—even prides itself on—promoting personal freedom, individuality, and independence. Recently, while visiting a refugee camp in Nigeria with a mixture of Muslims and Christians, I asked a local Christian pastor if the camp was able to feed all the people. His answer surprised me. He said the Muslims there do not view food as something owned by them. They eat outside their homes and gladly share with anyone walking by. Consequently, they always had enough food. The difficulty lay in getting some of the Christians to share.

As you travel around the globe, you will find that most Muslims are very hospitable. Many will even go into debt to provide food for a visitor. This way of relating to guests stands in stark contrast to the American promotion of personal independence and rights. It is no wonder many Muslims see America and Christianity as individualistic and self-centered.

Christians: Promoters of Violence

It is common knowledge that the United States spends more money on its military than any other country. In fact, America spends more on its armed forces than the next seven countries combined. What do you think this looks like to the rest of the world? Add up the total military expenditures in 2014 of China, Russia, Saudi Arabia, France, England, India, and Germany. Believe it or not, America spent more than all of those countries combined.[1] For many, this alone is sufficient evidence that America (i.e. Christianity) is the number one promoter of violence in our world.

In addition, many look at the United States as a country that supports ruthless dictators when they're useful, overthrows them when they're not, and gives little thought to the many innocent lives destroyed in the process. They find it ironic that while American missiles protecting oil interests are flying over their heads, America is preaching democracy, peace, equality, and freedom for all. In the minds of many Muslims, this is hypocritical and deceitful.

Perhaps their opinion regarding America isn't correct, but we need to understand that this is a real perception.

Christians: Promoters of Immorality

To many Muslims, America is the world's leading exporter of sexual decadence and debauchery. And many see this moral corruption as the fruit of Christianity. Muslim leaders watch with grave concern as Hollywood continues to produce movies glorifying immorality, sexual promiscuity, and the baser instincts of society. They see women dressing provocatively and degrading themselves on the screen. Western men are portrayed as lacking basic self-control. Since America is the chief producer of this material, Christianity is seen as a dangerous threat to Muslim communities and a great evil that must be stopped.

Christians: Destroyers of the Family

Family is extremely important in most Eastern cultures. Fathers are respected as leaders, and the mother's role in the home is greatly valued. Grandparents and older relatives are esteemed highly, and great honor is associated with age and experience. This respect and reverence runs deep and is viewed as essential to healthy community life. In some Eastern countries, several generations live together under one roof, and care of the elderly is an important responsibility.

So what happens when someone raised in this setting first observes the disrespectful attitudes Western youth display toward their parents? Can you imagine the fears Muslim parents must feel as they send their children off to get an American education in a country where the elderly are shipped off to commercial nursing homes to get them out of the way? Can we comprehend why their greatest fear might be to hear that their children enjoy the independent ways of the West, or even worse, that they have chosen to become Christians?

Perspective

Proper perspective is indispensable. If we are going to understand the strong anti-American feelings held by many Muslims around the globe, we must try to walk in the sandals of people like Bashir and put on their glasses. Not all of their perceptions may be correct, but we should at least try to see ourselves from their perspective. It could make a difference in how we respond to them.

CHAPTER FOUR

Islam from a Western Perspective

Of course, Muslims are not the only ones who are alarmed in this clash of cultures. As we saw earlier, many living in the West have grave concerns about Muslims as well. Terrorist attacks like the 2013 Boston marathon bombing seem to be increasing. In a survey conducted in the aftermath of the San Bernardino shootings by two radical Muslims, researchers found that 94 percent of all American adults see mass shootings as a critical issue.[1] Just four years prior, only 53 percent saw this as an important concern. Fear is on the rise.

On December 7, 2015, during the run-up to the 2016 presidential election, candidate Donald Trump capitalized on this fear. A campaign press release announced, "Donald J. Trump is calling for a total and complete shutdown of Muslims entering the United States until our country's representatives can figure out what is going on."[2] Many Americans, forgetting that this country has prided itself on religious inclusion, agreed.

In the last chapter we looked at the perceptions many Muslims have about American Christians. Let's look more closely at some of the perceptions Americans have about Muslims.

Muslims = Terrorists

Many Christians in America see the Islamic faith as violent. In December 2015, a poll of 1,003 adults was taken across all fifty states to determine the connection between violence and religious affiliation. Seventy-five percent of Americans polled said that people who call themselves Christians, yet commit violent crimes, are not really Christian. In contrast, only half of those polled believed that self-proclaimed Muslims who commit violent crimes are not actually Muslim.[3] In other words,

Americans believe Islam is a more violent religion than Christianity.

American Muslims have expended a great deal of money and energy to convince the West that their fears are unfounded, that the Islamic faith is actually a peace-loving religion. However, it is difficult to combat videos of jets flying into buildings, school children being taught to hate America, or women being publically flogged because they were too near to men. These images are powerful. As long as perpetrators of violence say they are killing in the name of Allah, many Americans will fear Muslims.

Islam: A Different Set of Values

In November 2015, political commentator and television host Bill Maher made the following observation: "There are many, many Muslim countries that either have sharia law or want sharia law. Those values are *not* our values."[4]

According to Maher, Muslims hold beliefs that are very different from American values. Recently I received an email from a friend living in a Muslim-majority country. He recently converted to Christianity, and his parents are now threatening to kill him. Americans are not used to this kind of response when a child converts to a different religion. Disappointment, yes, but violence? Consequently, Americans tend to suspect that the tenets driving the Islamic faith are, at some foundational level, different from "life, liberty, and the pursuit of happiness."[5]

Islam: A Religion with Global Ambitions

Many Westerners are concerned as they observe Islam's rapid growth. According to projections, the number of Muslims will nearly equal the number of Christians around the world by 2050. By then, Muslims will make up 10 percent of the overall population in Europe and will pass Judaism as the second largest religion in the United States.[6] The primary reason for this rapid increase is high fertility rates in developing Muslim-majority countries. But this growth contributes to the perception that the world is being overtaken by Islam and that Muslims have an eye on global dominance.

Western Europe has seen a great influx in Muslim immigration. In May 2016, Sadiq Khan, a British Muslim, was elected mayor of London. Amazing! Who would have ever dreamed even twenty years ago that London, headquarters of the Church of

England, would elect a Muslim mayor? But demographics are shifting. America's larger cities have also seen huge growth in their Muslim populations, and many are not pleased. When people see more Muslim neighbors, hear of increased violence on the streets, and believe there is a connection between the two, they become troubled.

With the Muslim faith growing faster than Christianity, Americans are afraid there will be ramifications on Election Day. What if the time comes when the majority of people casting votes are driven by a radically different set of values? What if a majority would like to see the United States controlled by sharia law rather than the Constitution?

At this point we are just addressing perceptions. Whether or not you see a direct connection between violence and the Muslim faith depends on your own experience and source of information. Maybe Americans have incorrect perceptions. After all, according to one poll, 83 percent of Americans say they know little or nothing about the religious practices and beliefs of Muslims, and 62 percent say they seldom or never have discussions with anyone they know to be a Muslim.[7] Are American fears grounded in reality? And if they are, what should followers of Jesus do?

How Should Christians Respond?

For a moment, let's assume that Western fears are warranted. Let's assume that the perceived threat of Islamic dominance is real, and in spite of what the polls tell us, most Muslims desire violence. And let's go even further. Let's imagine that there is a secret plot to take over America's way of life and value system. Let's even assume there is a sinister plan in place for radical Muslims to dominate the United States government, and that this hostile takeover appears imminent.

How should Christians in America respond? Would a follower of Jesus protest and try to prevent more Muslims from entering this country? Is this his civic duty? To answer these questions, we need to look at Jesus' life, since He is the one we profess to follow. How would He respond to a government that loves violence and cruelty?

CHAPTER FIVE

What Did Jesus Do?

A popular saying in Christian circles has been, "What would Jesus do?" But an often-neglected yet vital question is, "What *did* Jesus do?" If we are to know how Jesus would respond to a violent Islamic government, we must look at how He responded to similar situations in His day. Understanding the setting and political climate in which He lived will make it easier to grasp important truths that can help us comprehend how He would respond to radical Islam today.

There are many blessings in growing up within an atmosphere of democracy. Those of us living in the United States have experienced a stable government, a relatively good economy, and a (usually) peaceful political process. Leaders are elected according to a specific schedule, and though politicians promise more than they can deliver, there is a certain confidence that the populace is ultimately in control.

It is almost impossible for us to imagine living under a sovereign king or dictator who has the power to make major decisions with impunity. Imagine your state governor issuing an order to execute everyone in your city who refuses to join his political party. Or suppose the mayor of your town decides that those who do not align with his particular religious denomination can no longer shop within the city limits. Our indignation flares and our thoughts race. *That is ridiculously unfair! Just who does he think he is?*

But Jesus lived in exactly such a setting. Shortly after His birth, Herod the Great sent soldiers through Bethlehem and the surrounding area to kill all the children two years old and under.[a] Why? Because he felt threatened.

Can you fathom this kind of power? A local ruler sending troops through your town to slaughter all the toddlers just because he feels like it? That is the kind of power kings have. In reality, the situation was even more complex. Herod represented the

---

[a] Matthew 2:13–18

power of a foreign invader, and from the Jews' perspective, he didn't even belong there. Rome made the life of the average Jew very difficult. I am sure Jesus grew up hearing heated conversations as local men and religious leaders expounded on the evils of Rome while glancing over their shoulders, hoping they weren't overheard.

But the Jews remembered a different time—a time when Israel had been known throughout the world as a power to be reckoned with, when rulers like the Queen of Sheba came from far away just to gaze at Israel's splendor. Those were the glory days!

Now the Jewish people, Jesus' people, were ruled by a ruthless, corrupt, unjust government. The Romans had no respect for God's Word or His laws. They were an extremely cruel regime, famous for conquering and killing without mercy. In short, Jesus grew up in an environment much like the type of government many Americans fear. He saw the oppression of the common people. He was familiar with heavy taxation on the poor to facilitate newer palaces and better living conditions for the Roman elite. Jesus saw no representation in the electoral process and knew the impossibility of the common man expressing an opposing view. There was no freedom of speech. If you weren't a Roman, you could be executed without a trial. Jesus' own cousin, John the Baptist, had been imprisoned and beheaded for speaking the truth. The freedoms Americans have grown up with were available to only a select few, and Jesus' people were excluded. This is the setting Jesus lived in.

There came a day when Jesus finally had the opportunity to make things right. He was popular with the masses, political opinion was united against Rome, and His people were ready to make Him king. The Jewish people had been longing for this moment. Surely someone who could make the blind see, enable the lame to walk, and even raise dead people to life could easily liberate them from Rome. Jesus was their man. Here was their chance!

What Did Jesus Do?

So how did Jesus respond to this corrupt government with its unethical leaders? How did He handle this unprecedented chance to bring about political change?

Amazingly, as we know but often forget, Jesus didn't focus on the politics of His day. Incredible as it may seem, He never even spoke against the abuses of the Roman government. Open your Bible and read through His teachings. Where is the outcry against the exploitation and human rights abuses of the day? People repeatedly assumed He was about to overthrow the Roman government, yet nothing happened. He had the power and the political capital, but the call for civil revolution never came. Many Jews were likely disappointed after public gatherings where He had been the keynote speaker. Can't you hear them as they head back home?

"The same thing happened again! He speaks of love and caring for the poor. He talks about a kingdom where everyone shares and where God takes care of our natural needs. That is what we desperately need. But with Rome in power, what can we do? This Jesus talks like the king we need, but He doesn't actually do anything!"

I suspect many disillusioned people trudged home, thinking, *Another day, more about this kingdom, a few healings, and still He does nothing about the real problem of Rome.* The Jewish leaders were aware of Jesus' silence on this important topic. One day they asked Him, "Is it lawful for us to pay taxes to Caesar or not?"[b] It was a good question. Was it really right for them to pay taxes and fund

---

[b] Luke 20:22

this ruthless regime? But notice His answer. "Render therefore to Caesar the things that are Caesar's, and to God the things that are God's."[c]

Astounding! No comment about the central concern of the day. Just encouragement to pay taxes to the earthly kingdom they were under, and a hint about this other kingdom of God that they had a responsibility to as well.

But was Jesus doing nothing? Did He really ignore the Roman subjugators? The book of Matthew describes another dramatic encounter with the powers of Rome. This time it was with a centurion. And while this one seemed to be more upright than most, centurions were the face of the cruel Roman government. These men forced the will of Rome on the Jewish people. Remember, we want to know how Jesus would respond to an unfair and corrupt government. So for a moment picture this centurion as a radical Islamic leader. How did Jesus respond to the face of this oppressive power?

---

[c] Luke 20:25

The Power of Love

The centurion's servant was sick and grievously tormented, and the centurion came seeking help. The Bible says Jesus marveled at the centurion's faith, saying that this Roman commander had more faith than anyone He had met in Israel. He then told him to go back, and his servant would be restored. When the centurion arrived home, he found his servant healed.[d]

The Jews must have been incredulous. No lashing out at Roman aggression, no outburst for brutal crimes the centurion had committed, and not a word about Roman occupation. Nothing! Jesus treated this Roman soldier just like every other needy person He encountered—with love and compassion.

Jesus was fully capable of delivering verbal thrashings, and we find Him doing just that to the Jewish leaders of His day.[e] He was also able to bluntly address the hypocrisy of the errant Jewish lawyers.[f] But when confronted with a basic need, even though the centurion represented the opposing political force

---

[d] Matthew 8:5–13
[e] Matthew 23
[f] Luke 11:46

of His time, Jesus met that need with kindness.

Notice the consistent testimony of Jesus' interaction with this Roman regime. When asked about paying taxes, Jesus was clear. His followers were to pay taxes to the earthly government in power, even if that administration was ruthless and cruel. And when confronted with human need, they were to show kindness, even if the person in need happened to be a Roman leader.

How would Jesus respond to a radical Islamic government? Just like He would to a centurion—with love and compassion. And such a response continues to be a trademark of His kingdom.

CHAPTER SIX

Jesus' Overriding Message

Are you puzzled by the fact that Jesus made no verbal attack on the Roman government of His day? No political statements, pleas to Rome about human rights abuses, or public calls for a regime change? Does it seem strange that Jesus encouraged paying taxes and even healed the servant of one of their soldiers? Does the thought seem bizarre that Jesus, if He were living in America today, might not be overly concerned about the country being overtaken by Islamic radicals?

These are difficult questions. Maybe we need to go back and take another look at the life and interactions of Jesus. Is it possible that we have missed His overriding message? Do we really understand the Man we say we follow?

Do not underestimate the oppressiveness of

Roman occupation. It was the hot topic of the day. Even after all Jesus' teaching, His death on the cross, and His triumphant resurrection from the dead, the question on the minds of those closest to Him just before He ascended hadn't changed: "Lord, will you at this time restore the kingdom to Israel?"[a] This oppressive and domineering government was a constant reality. Here the disciples were, just a few moments from Jesus' ascension. Was Jesus just going to ignore this painful problem?

But Jesus had something more powerful than Roman occupation on His mind. He had preached a consistent message for three and a half years, but they seemed to have missed it.

As we listen to modern Christianity and consider the messages being preached across American pulpits, one has to stop and ask: Have we missed His message as well? What was the primary theme of Jesus' ministry?

Jesus' Primary Theme: The Kingdom of God

If you were to identify the primary message Jesus preached, what would it be? Many would say, "Jesus

---

[a] Acts 1:6

came to die for our sins and save us from hell." Of course, Jesus did speak about salvation, but actually only a few times. Others might say, "Jesus' primary theme was the new birth." Again, being born again is very important, but Jesus spoke specifically on this topic only once.

We are familiar with Jesus' teachings recorded in the Gospels. He talked about things like the importance of prayer and how to pray, and He gave us a lot of instruction about money and how to regard it. Jesus talked about the afterlife and told many parables showing the importance of living with an eternal perspective. But there is a topic He focused on much more than these.

The clear, consistent theme of Jesus' teaching was the kingdom of God. Repeatedly we read passages like this one: "From that time Jesus began to preach and to say, 'Repent, for the kingdom of heaven is at hand.' "[b] Just a little later in the same chapter, "Jesus went about all Galilee, teaching in their synagogues, preaching the gospel of the kingdom, and healing all kinds of sickness and all kinds of disease among the people."[c]

---

[b] Matthew 4:17
[c] Matthew 4:23

Jesus seemed preoccupied with this kingdom. There are over one hundred references to it throughout the four Gospels. When He sent disciples out to preach, He told them to go out and preach the kingdom of God.[d] This "gospel of the kingdom" permeates the teachings of Jesus. Isn't it remarkable that we hear so little about it? Much of the focus in our churches today is man's salvation and what Jesus said about our personal relationship with Him. But His primary, over-riding theme was consistently the kingdom of God.

Why was Jesus so focused on this kingdom? Again, remember the backdrop against which Jesus was preaching. Instead of focusing on the Roman Empire and its evils, His focus was on a glorious kingdom that He had come to herald. Perhaps getting a clearer picture of the beauty of this kingdom will help us understand why Jesus wasn't that interested in Roman occupation—and why He might not be too concerned if a radical Islamic regime was on the political horizon.

A Glorious Kingdom

Get a picture of the magnificent kingdom Jesus

---

[d] Matthew 10:7, Luke 9:2 and 10:9

was visualizing and proclaiming. Imagine a society where people love others the way they love themselves, where they tenderly care for their sick, elderly, and handicapped. Visualize a setting where material poverty bears no stigma and where caring for the homeless is normal. Think of a kingdom where the King lovingly watches over His citizens, and there is no reason to worry or anxiously store up money against future unknowns.

Try to imagine what it would be like to live in a setting where citizens love to share anonymously so that their King receives all the glory. Picture those with financial struggles mysteriously finding cash in blank envelopes or discovering food in their pantries that they didn't purchase.

It's hard, but visualize a kingdom where honesty prevails and swearing to tell nothing but the truth is pointless. A kingdom where a man's word is his bond, and the need for lawyers is a fading memory. What a place to live!

Can you comprehend a society where love flows everywhere you look? Husbands love their wives, children love and obey their parents, and most astonishing of all, people love even the enemies of this kingdom. What a beautiful sight!

This was how Jesus described this kingdom He had come to proclaim. And He planned to set up this magnificent kingdom of light right in the middle of the world of darkness He lived in.

Dream with me for a moment and try to see what Jesus saw: a kingdom, or subculture if you will, radically different from surrounding culture. Small church communities all around the globe daily demonstrating what the entire world could look like if everyone followed Jesus.

"By this all will know that you are My disciples," Jesus said before He went back to the Father, "if you have love for one another."[e] Today there is a huge emphasis on tracts, missions, and billboards in an effort to spread the Gospel. But what would happen if the church were again known for self-denying love? Not only love for the lost, but love for each other?

Jesus came to a broken world—a world of broken

---

[e] John 13:35

promises, broken relationships, and broken trust. It was a self-centered world where people seemed to pursue only things that benefited or brought pleasure to themselves—much like the setting we experience today. But in contrast, Jesus described His kingdom as a place where love for God and others is primary, and where those highly esteemed are those who serve others best.[f]

Who wouldn't want to live in such a kingdom? Only a fool would turn away from an opportunity to live in a setting like this. Jesus came not just to save individuals from their sins and provide a ticket to a future place called heaven, but to usher in a present kingdom right here on the earth. That was His mission.

So what happened to this kingdom? We look around at professing Christianity and sometimes see little resemblance to this magnificent empire Jesus described. What happened to this glorious kingdom He came to set up? Did it slowly decay over the centuries? Was it a good idea but just too radical and idealistic to endure? How did it impact the powerful and ruthless Roman Empire?

---

[f] Matthew 20:25–27

CHAPTER SEVEN

The Kingdom and the Early Church

Immediately following Jesus' resurrection and ascension, the disciples spread throughout the Roman Empire, preaching as they went. Following the example of their Master, they said little about Rome's corruption, exploitations, or brutality. They simply taught that believers should pray for their government leaders,[a] honor them,[b] and obey them whenever possible.[c]

Those first believers operated in the shadow of this powerful Roman government, and they understood firsthand the cruel tyranny a totalitarian regime is capable of unleashing. But just like Jesus,

---

[a] 1 Timothy 2:1–2
[b] 1 Peter 2:17
[c] Romans 13:1–7

they seemed somewhat indifferent to its abuses. They just continued preaching the same message Jesus had preached. It was a theme they were excited about: the message of the kingdom.

We read of Philip preaching "the things concerning the kingdom of God and the name of Jesus Christ."[d] We also read of Paul going into synagogues, "reasoning and persuading concerning the things of the kingdom of God."[e] Their preaching revolved around the power of the Resurrection and the kingdom Jesus had brought. They obviously believed this kingdom held the answers to man's deepest needs.

A Present and Powerful Reality

This kingdom wasn't a far-off utopia; it was a present reality. A man became a citizen immediately upon choosing to follow Christ, and it required total commitment. When a man chose to turn his back on earthly kingdoms and become part of this kingdom of Jesus Christ, unconditional allegiance was a prerequisite.

This shouldn't be difficult for us to understand.

---

[d] Acts 8:12
[e] Acts 19:8

It is impossible to give unreserved loyalty to two countries at the same time. One citizenship must be preeminent.

The kingdom of God is no different. Only those who are willing to pledge unconditional allegiance to Jesus and His kingdom can be His disciples.[f] Yet despite Jesus' clear teaching, it seems professing Christians have spent the greater part of the last two thousand years trying to prove Him wrong. Repeatedly men have tried to pledge allegiance to constitutions, earthly kingdoms, and armed forces of various countries while claiming to follow Jesus. But it wasn't always this way. Those first Christians understood that choosing to become part of Christ's kingdom meant disavowing the claims of all others.

But shouldn't good men who are followers of Jesus be chosen to oversee our earthly governments? Wouldn't the church want men who are faithful to the Bible to fill government administrative roles? This question was asked many years ago of the early Christians. Celsus was a second-century Greek philosopher and an opponent of Christianity. He proposed that if the Christians believed earthly

[f] Luke 14:33

governments would benefit from their involvement, then Christians should aspire to administrative positions. But Origen, an early Christian writer, defended the church's stance of avoiding participation in earthly governments. Take note of his response: "It is not for the purpose of escaping public duties that Christians decline public offices, but that they may reserve themselves for a diviner and more necessary service in the Church of God—for the salvation of men."[1]

Those first Christians were so excited about this kingdom of God that they had no interest in giving allegiance to anything else. This was alarming to the Roman government (as it is to many governments today). When they discovered that Christians wouldn't pledge allegiance to the Emperor, they chased them, tortured them, and fed them to lions. The Christians' allegiance was pledged to a kingdom that focused on peace, not violence, and on inner beauty rather than outward adornment. Their focus was on loving God and other people, not on entertainment or fulfillment of selfish desires. It was a kingdom that cared for the poor, the marginalized, and the outcast, where men chose to live simply so they could better help those in need. And they were willing to die rather than compromise!

An Unstoppable Kingdom

The Romans didn't know what to do with people like this. They wouldn't fight. They were indifferent to worldly honors and unmoved by temporal wealth. It seemed no matter

Marcellus, a Roman centurion stationed in Spain, was arrested in 298 A.D. for throwing down his sword in front of the flag during a military parade after his conversion. When challenged in court, Marcellus declared, "It is not fitting that a Christian, who fights for Christ his Lord, should be a soldier according to the brutalities of this world." As a result, Marcellus was executed by the sword.[2]

how hard Rome tried to stamp them out, they continued to infiltrate the empire. Rome had subdued many powerful regimes, but they didn't know what to do with a kingdom of love.

The fire of Christianity spread across the Roman Empire, and we still marvel at what God was able to accomplish through those early Christians. They faced a foe as fierce as any radical Islamic regime—and conquered! The Christianity of that time was truly a powerful kingdom that turned the world of their day upside down![g]

A Kingdom with Purpose

God always has a purpose behind His actions, and throughout Scripture God reveals two primary purposes in His interaction with men. One is to demonstrate His glory, and the other is to reconcile people (His creation) unto Himself. So how does this kingdom fit into God's plan?

God has always desired a people who would demonstrate His glory. He didn't bless Israel in the Old Testament just so they could all enjoy an easy life of plenty. No, God wanted Israel to be a public, corporate demonstration of God's power and beauty. He wanted surrounding nations to look at the nation of Israel and see what the entire world could be like if everyone followed Him.

Notice Psalm 67. "God be merciful to us and bless us, and cause His face to shine upon us."[h] This is a prayer asking God to pour out wealth

---

[g] Acts 17:6
[h] Psalm 67:1

and prosperity on the nation of Israel. But why? So every Israelite could live happily and retire young? No, notice the next verse. "That Your way may be known on earth, Your salvation among all nations."[i] God wasn't interested in only this one country. His ultimate desire was to pour blessing on all nations. Israel was being asked to provide a public demonstration of God's intent for the entire world!

Today, followers of Jesus play this same role. The kingdom Jesus was preaching is to be a present reality. There is more coming, to be sure, but this kingdom is to demonstrate His glory right now in the midst of a hurting world. What an amazing opportunity for the church of Jesus Christ to corporately exhibit the beauty of the King!

---

[i] Psalm 67:2

CHAPTER EIGHT

"I Would Love to Meet People Like That!"

I first met Samira[a] at an interfaith meeting at our local university. People of several faiths had been invited to share why they believed and practiced as they did. Samira was one of the speakers that evening. Wearing a hijab, she told of growing up as a refugee in a Middle Eastern country. She was very aware of different religions. There were both Christians and Muslims in her extended family, and she made a choice at a young age to follow Islam. Now here she stood in an American university, the most modestly dressed woman in the room, sharing how much her Islamic faith meant to her. Samira intrigued me.

---

[a] Name has been changed to protect privacy.

She had uncles who had converted from Islam to Christianity, a father who had traded Marxism for Islam, and other family members who didn't profess any religious belief at all. She had traveled the world and lived in both American Christian homes and in Muslim communities. If there was ever a young girl free to make up her own mind about religion, it was Samira, and she had chosen to follow Muhammad. Why?

After the meeting I contacted Samira and arranged for an interview. She told me her story. Her parents were Palestinian but were living in a Lebanese refugee camp when she was born. Her mother was raised Christian, while her father was born into a Muslim family. About half of her mother's family were Christians. Her father had first professed faith in Jesus, but later converted from Christianity to Marxism after studying economics in a communist country. Later, after communism's fall from favor in many parts of the world, he converted to Islam. Samira remembers seeing the local imam come into their home when she was a small child and teach her father how to pray.

While she was in fifth grade, Samira decided to wear the Muslim hijab. She had been the only girl in her class who didn't, and she said the choice was primarily a result of peer pressure. Samira's parents never tried to influence her religious choices. She doesn't remember them ever sitting down with her and discussing spiritual things. Her father wanted her to belong to some religion, but didn't want her to become too radical. So her religious beliefs were primarily formed by her friends.

Time to Decide

When Samira was sixteen, she had an opportunity to travel abroad for schooling. For two years she lived in Italy with a Christian family while advancing her education, and then she moved to the United States to attend college. Still a follower of Islam, she was again placed in a Christian home. Each Sunday she attended church with her host family, while in private devotions she read the Quran.

"I realized I had become a Muslim simply because of peer pressure. But I knew when I moved away from home it was time for me to decide what I really believed."

Samira tried to analyze the differences she saw in religions. She has observed Muslims who were honest and others who were not. But she could say the same about Jews and Christians. So how could she decide which religion was actually true?

Samira was refreshingly honest about herself. When asked why she chose to follow Islam, she said, "To be honest, I'm Muslim because I grew up in a Muslim community. If we had stayed in a Christian city, I believe I would be a Christian today."

So for the past several years Samira has been hitting all the bases. She worships with Muslims on Fridays, goes to synagogue on Saturdays, and attends a Christian church on Sundays. And since I wanted to know why, after all this exposure, she was still a Muslim, I asked for her perspective on American Christianity.

Samira's Observations

Growing up as a Palestinian refugee in Lebanon, Samira had heard a lot about America, and most of it wasn't good. She had viewed Muslims as pursuers of peace and the United States as violent and trying to take over the world. Her perception of

America was that it was famous for three things: wealth, movies, and military might. Because of this, she concluded that Americans were probably not religious or friendly to foreigners.

Upon arriving in America, Samira found that some of her assumptions were correct and some were totally false. She was shocked to find such friendly people. Her Christian host family was caring and hospitable. They showed an interest in her life and invited her to their church. She had assumed Americans were not religious and was surprised to find many attending worship services each Sunday.

There were also some disappointments. "When I went to church, the people were all very friendly at first. But after a couple Sundays I was asked if I agreed with their teaching. I told them I believed in Jesus as a prophet, but didn't believe in the Trinity or Resurrection. So guess what I heard about for the next three Sundays." She laughed. "That is right, lessons on why God is three persons and why the Resurrection is true."

People assumed Samira was ignorant of Christian theology. They seemed confident that as soon as Christianity had been sufficiently explained, she would convert. Some even asked if she was ready now to take that scarf off and get baptized. When she wasn't ready, relationships cooled rapidly. People who had been friendly began to distance themselves from her. She was rejecting their religion, and they were rejecting her.

"I found this very painful and would ask them, 'Is this the way your Jesus teaches you to do? To only be friendly until you see people aren't going to convert?' "

Samira also noticed other things about American Christians. She knew enough about Jesus' teachings to know what He taught about divorce and remarriage.[b] But she saw American churches ignoring this teaching. She read passages in the Bible that taught modesty and simplicity,[c] yet these professing followers of Jesus spent more time and money on their hair and makeup than women in the Muslim communities she grew up in. But one thing was even more amazing to Samira. She knew that Jesus had stressed the importance of loving your enemies and turning the other cheek.[d] She knew He had taught

---

[b] Mark 10:11–12
[c] 1 Peter 3:1–4
[d] Matthew 5:38, 39, 44

a nonviolent way of life. Yet as she listened to her host family talk around the dinner table, she heard about the importance of fighting and supporting the military. They seemed proud of America's military might and global involvement.

Samira's Impression

Samira's overall impression of Americans was positive. She found them to be friendly, caring, and willing to share. When she found herself in a financial difficulty shortly after moving, her host family's church heard about the problem, held a fundraiser, and shared their resources with her. Her general impression of American Christians was that they were nice people.

On the other hand, she could say the same about her Muslim community in Lebanon. They were also friendly, caring, and willing to share when people had difficulties. In fact, where she came from, community was emphasized more than in American churches she observed. So far, Samira had seen nothing to convince her to convert to Christianity.

"When I first came to America, I was searching for truth. I wanted to know what was right. But the closer I got to Christianity, the more I realized it wasn't what I wanted for my life. Nice people, but they don't seem to have a better religion."

So what does Samira want? This sincere young woman is obviously still searching for something. Anyone who would attend a mosque on Friday, a synagogue on Saturday, and a Christian church on Sunday is a serious seeker. So what is she looking for?

"I Would Love to Meet People Like That!"

Finishing our interview, I described the first Christian believers and their view of the kingdom of God. I shared how they lived and how radically different the early church was from what she has observed in America.

I asked Samira, "Have you ever met a group of people who actually try to follow the teachings of Jesus? People who, like Jesus, put the welfare of others above their own and attempt to treat others as they want to be treated? People who refuse to fight and whose goal is to show love to their enemies? Have you ever met people who would rather die themselves than take the life of another?"

We were sitting around a coffee table in the student lounge, and I can still picture the look on her face as she leaned forward in her chair. "That is different than the Christianity I have seen. I would love to meet people like that! I would love to meet them. But I haven't!"

Sadly, Samira and many other Muslims are still searching for authentic kingdom Christianity.

CHAPTER NINE

Two Kingdoms

Earlier we looked at the beauty of this kingdom Jesus visualized. But much of His teaching focused on the great cost required of those who would enter. While most revolutionaries give great assurance and make extensive promises, Jesus did just the opposite. From the beginning of His ministry, He stated unequivocally that joining His kingdom could cause one to be ostracized,[a] unpopular, and part of a minority movement.[b] What kind of a leader would attempt a revolution by telling potential followers they could expect misery and rejection? Imagine starting a movement by saying, "Come join my kingdom; all are welcome! But understand, you

---

[a] Luke 6:22–23
[b] Matthew 10:22

will have conflict in your family,[c] be hated by your neighbors,[d] and experience persecution from religious leaders and government authorities!"[e]

Most would-be leaders tell the advantages, even overselling the possibilities with glowing promises. But not Jesus. He was brutally honest and crystal clear that only the serious need apply. It was a magnificent kingdom, but it wasn't a cushy lifestyle for the faint of heart.

Jesus never promised immediate world dominance. Instead He spoke of coming difficulties, betrayal, and persecution, promising reward only to the few who held out to the end.[f] For a time, it was going to be a minority kingdom within a larger culture. Its citizens were to bless others, share with them, and show a better way.

Not of This World?

Jesus was clear that His kingdom wasn't going to be the only kingdom on the earth. Two kingdoms existed simultaneously, and Jesus said His kingdom was going to be very different. Notice these

[c] Mathew 10:36; Luke 12:53
[d] Mark 13:13
[e] Matthew 10:18
[f] Matthew 24:13; Revelation 2:10

startling words of Jesus just before His crucifixion: "My kingdom is not of this world. If My kingdom were of this world, My servants would fight."[g] What kind of empire has human subjects, yet refuses to use force? A kingdom whose citizens refuse to fight? How would such a kingdom interact with an earthly kingdom that does fight? How, for example, would such a kingdom respond to radical Islam? Fortunately, we have writings from the early Christians to help with these questions. Remember, those first believers understood what it was like to live under a cruel regime. Even more, many had the advantage of talking with those who had personally been with Jesus!

For the first several hundred years after Jesus' ascension, the early Christians were known for their refusal to take up arms. Of course, they had many critics. The Romans viewed this refusal to fight as foolish. They argued that good men must rise up and fight or evil would prevail. In response to one of these pagan Romans, the early writer Origen said, "As we by our prayers vanquish all demons who stir up war, and lead to the violation of oaths,

---

[g] John 18:36

and disturb the peace, we are in this way much more helpful to the kings than those who go into the field to fight for them."

Notice, even though Christians were not willing to disobey Jesus by going out and fighting, they were still active in the battle—by praying! Origen explains further, "None fight better for the king than we do. We do not fight under him, although he require it; but we fight on his behalf, forming a special army—an army of piety—by offering our prayers to God."[1]

These first believers understood that evil can never be overcome by more evil. Violence begets violence, and we see this today firsthand in the Middle East. Each time a missile is launched across a border, the receiving side feels obligated to strike back. Back and forth, this retaliation has been going on for years, leaving an aftermath of anger, hatred, and needless carnage.

But Jesus brought a different way, and those first Christians were known for responding with love. Athenagoras, a writer who lived in the middle of the second century, wrote, "We have learned, not only not to return blow for blow . . . but to those who smite us on the one side of the face to offer the other side also, and to those who take away our coat to give likewise our cloak."[2]

Athenagoras wrote this to the Roman Emperor, trying to explain the difference between the kingdom of God and the kingdoms of this world. Earthly governments are governed by force, while the kingdom of Jesus Christ is ruled by love. This kingdom, referred to so many times in Scripture, has both a future and present sense to it. The Apostle Peter speaks of someday entering "into the everlasting kingdom of our Lord and Savior Jesus Christ."[h] That is a time every believer looks forward to. But the apostles' primary focus and message was its present reality. These followers of Jesus remembered well His very first sermon. "The time is fulfilled, and the kingdom of God is at hand. Repent and believe in the gospel."[i] It is a real and present kingdom, with

---

[h] 2 Peter 1:11
[i] Mark 1:15

real citizens and a glorious King.

The Two-Kingdom View

So what happened to the original belief in two kingdoms? For many years Christians were famous for refusing to take up the sword and for loving their enemies as Jesus had taught.[j] Following Jesus' example, the Apostle Paul encouraged the church at Corinth to "bless those who persecute you."[k] Later, the Apostle Peter also taught the early church not to "return evil for evil or reviling for reviling."[l] This was the accepted teaching and the historic doctrine of the early church.

But looking around at professing Christians today, you would think that Jesus and the apostles had never opened their mouths regarding this topic. The early church was known for declining powerful positions in government and for promoting peace. The evangelical church of America is known for chasing political power and supporting candidates who promote an expanded military. It is more famous for political power than for spiritual

---

[j] Matthew 5:44
[k] Romans 12:14
[l] 1 Peter 3:9

power. It is a religion those first followers of Jesus wouldn't recognize. But imagine what might happen if Christianity returned to the original vision and teachings of its Founder!

CHAPTER TEN

How Would Jesus Respond?

It really isn't difficult to know how Jesus or the early church would respond to radical Islam, since we know how they responded to a similar situation in their day. Even though Jesus was innocent of any crime, He chose love instead of retaliation when accused and punished. He demonstrated by His life, death, and resurrection that love is more powerful than violence and hate.

You may be thinking, *Jesus did this because He had a specific mission, but it is different for Christians. Surely Jesus doesn't intend for us to just let people walk over us!*

In the last chapter we looked at some words written by the Apostle Peter. If there was ever a man qualified to speak on this issue, it must be him. Peter certainly wasn't afraid to defend himself. He was the impulsive disciple who verbalized his desire to follow Jesus to the end and proved his zeal by wielding his sword in the Garden of Gethsemane.[a] But after taking a swing at Malchus's head,

> He was just twenty-one years old, but when recruited by the Roman army, Maximilian knew how followers of Jesus should respond. Standing before the proconsul, he boldly announced, "I cannot enlist; I cannot serve; I cannot do evil. I am a Christian!"
>
> The proconsul continued, "You must serve or die!"
>
> "You can cut off my head," Maximilian calmly replied, "but I will not be a soldier of this world. I am a soldier of Jesus Christ!" Maximilian was beheaded for his faith March 12, A.D. 295.[1]

being rebuked by Jesus, and observing Jesus' death and resurrection, notice these words to his fellow believers years later:

> For to this you were called, because Christ also suffered for us, leaving us an example, that you should follow His steps: Who

---

[a] John 18:10

committed no sin, nor was deceit found in His mouth; who, when He was reviled, did not revile in return; when He suffered, He did not threaten, but committed Himself to Him who judges righteously.[b]

Did you catch that? The way Jesus responded is to be a pattern for us to follow! Stop for a moment and consider both this statement and the man who said it.

What happened to the blustery, combative, take-charge Peter who wasn't about to let anyone run over him? What happened to the man who believed the kingdom could be advanced and protected by the sword? The old Peter had been transformed! He finally glimpsed this new kingdom Jesus had been proclaiming—not an earthly kingdom that uses swords, hate, and military might, but a kingdom that conquers by love. A kingdom whose citizens forgive, love, and bless their enemies.

Today's Christianity
Today's Christianity is very similar to the old Peter.

---

[b] 1 Peter 2:21–23

It likes to talk about grace, forgiveness, and love. It likes to be known for following Jesus and having a relationship with Him. It loves to tell how powerful Jesus is and be associated with His program. But when opposition appears on the horizon, today's Christianity reaches for the sword.

> For we no longer take up the sword against nations, nor do we learn war anymore, having become children of peace, for the sake of Jesus, who is our leader. —Origen [2]

Modern Christianity is famous for saying great things and promoting great themes. It is long on seminars, webinars, and radio talk shows about love, but short on demonstrating what Jesus taught. It continually churns out more material about grace but isn't known for exhibiting it. Its pulpits, websites, and bookstores proclaim lofty themes, but the daily lives of professing Christians bear a close resemblance to their non-believing neighbors. Christians seem to be saying great things, but not living them.

Early Christianity
But early Christianity was far different. In fact, it was exactly the opposite! Around A.D. 200 one

early Christian said, "We do not speak great things, but we live them!"[3] Today's Christianity would be laughed at for making that kind of claim, but the Romans didn't laugh when the early Christians said it. They knew it was true.

Those first believers were serious about following Jesus in daily life, not just knowing more about Him. They didn't relegate Jesus' teaching about loving their enemies (and they certainly had them) to Sunday school class. They applied it to their lives. They knew that following Jesus was costly, and many became lunch for the lions because of their unwavering stand. That was simply the cost of discipleship. They believed Jesus meant what He said, and they were determined, through His strength, to be faithful unto death.

This is a Christianity that Muslims like Samira have never seen. To them, America and Christianity are synonymous, not renowned for peace but for the largest military on the planet. But what if Christianity again became known for following Jesus? What if the church again became famous for loving its enemies? What if professing followers of Jesus actually started following Him?

There will always be earthly governments. God's

Word tells us that earthly governments are set up and even ordained by God.[c] But Jesus was also clear that there were going to be two kingdoms on this earth, and His would be different. His servants would not fight![d] And since that time there have always been men and women who have pledged allegiance only to the kingdom of Jesus Christ. They have believed that Jesus said what He meant and meant what He said. They have believed that love really is stronger than hate.

What will actually conquer this force known as radical Islam? Should Christians promote more bombs, guns, and grenades? More bloodshed, more slaughtered civilians, more villages blown apart? No.

---

[c] Romans 13:1–7
[d] John 18:36

Hate begets more hatred. Hate can only be conquered by sacrificial love, and love is the theme of the kingdom of Jesus Christ.

If you have questions or would like to locate other followers of Jesus who are serious about doing what He says, please contact kingdomquestions@gmail.com.

Endnotes

Chapter One

[1] <http://www.cnn.com/2014/08/19/world/meast/isis-james-foley/>, accessed on 2/22/16.

[2] <http://leaksource.info/2014/09/02/graphic-video-islamic-state-beheads-american-journalist-steven-sotloff/>, accessed on 2/22/16.

[3] <http://www.cnn.com/2014/09/08/politics/cnn-poll-isis/>, accessed on 2/23/16.

Chapter Three

[1] Peter G. Peterson Foundation, <http://www.pgpf.org/chart-archive/0053_defense-comparison>, accessed on 3/10/16.

Chapter Four

[1] <http://www.usatoday.com/story/news/2015/12/10/religion-news-service-poll-terrorism-shootings-muslims/77101070/>, accessed on 3/10/16.

[2] <http://www.cnn.com/2015/12/07/politics/donald-trump-muslim-ban-immigration/>, accessed on 3/10/16.

[3] <http://publicreligion.org/research/2015/12/survey-nearly-half-of-americans-worried-that-they-or-their-family-will-be-a-victim-of-terrorism/#ZugZcpwrKUm>, accessed on 3/15/16.

[4] <http://thefederalist.com/2015/11/21/bill-maher-blasts-liberals-for-believing-that-muslims-share-the-same-values/>, accessed on 3/15/16.

[5] The United States Declaration of Independence, July 4, 1776.

[6] <http://www.pewforum.org/2015/04/02/religious-projections-2010-2050/>, accessed on 3/15/16.

[7] <http://www.usatoday.com/story/news/2015/12/10/religion-news-service-poll-terrorism-shootings-muslims/77101070/>, accessed on 5/2/16.

Chapter Seven

[1] *Origen Against Celsus,* Book 8, Chapter 75, Ante-Nicene Fathers, Vol. IV, Eerdmans Publishing Company, Edinburgh, 1989, p. 668.

[2] Jean-Michel Hornus, *It Is Not Lawful for Me to Fight,* Wipf and Stock Publishers, Eugene, OR, 2009, p. 138.

Chapter Nine

[1] Ibid.

[2] Athenagoras the Athenian, *A Plea for the Christians,* Ante-Nicene Fathers, Vol. II, Eerdmans Publishing Company, Edinburgh, 1989, p. 129.

Chapter Ten

[1] <http://johnamills.com/faithstories/stmax.htm>, accessed on 3/30/16.

[2] *Origen Against Celsus,* Chapter 33, Ante-Nicene Fathers, Vol. IV, Eerdmans Publishing Company, Edinburgh, 1989, p. 558.

[3] *The Octavius of Minucius Felix,* Chapter 38, Ante-Nicene Fathers, Vol. IV, Eerdmans Publishing Company, Edinburgh, 1989, p. 197.

Resources for
Further Study

If you would like to learn more about the kingdom of God, the early Christians, or Islam, here are some additional resources you may want to consider.

The Kingdom That Turned the World Upside Down
David Bercot

This is an excellent work on the early church, their love for the kingdom of God, and how their devotion to Jesus impacted the Roman world. If you are serious about seeking God and learning about the early church, this is an extremely good resource.

The Upside-Down Kingdom
Donald B. Kraybill

The author explores the Lordship of Jesus and how

it should affect His people. It is a study of the kingdom of God through the Synoptic Gospels and contrasts the kingdom of this world with the kingdom of God.

A Change of Allegiance
Dean Taylor

The author and his wife were both enlisted in the U.S. Army when they began to realize what Jesus said about loving their enemies. This is a firsthand account of two people who seriously looked at applying the teachings of Jesus, knowing that choosing to follow would be costly. It is an excellent book to better understand defenseless living and the concept of two kingdoms.

How Christians Made Peace with War
John Driver

This book looks at the changes in history, specifically regarding the use of force. Jesus taught His followers to practice love and forgiveness. This book follows the theological changes across the centuries and shows how professing believers eventually became involved in military life.

Answering Jihad: A Better Way Forward
Nabeel Qureshi
(*author of* Seeking Allah, Finding Jesus)

Written by a former Muslim, the author addresses many questions surrounding the Islamic faith. He takes a close look at the origins of jihad and sharia law and explores why Muslims are being radicalized. The book also delves into whether Muslims and Christians worship the same God and what Jesus taught about violence. Though the author doesn't embrace a two-kingdom theology, he is honest with the teachings of Jesus regarding violence and how to best respond to radical Islam.

A Dictionary of Early Christian Beliefs
David Bercot

This dictionary can be helpful in learning what the early Christians believed regarding specific topics. Topics are in alphabetical order, and quotes are used so you can see what these early followers of Christ believed about each subject.

About the Author

Gary Miller was raised in California and today lives with his wife Patty and family in the Pacific Northwest. Gary works with the poor in developing countries and directs the SALT Microfinance Solutions program for Christian Aid Ministries. This program offers business and spiritual teaching to those living in chronic poverty, provides small loans, sets up local village savings groups, and assists them in learning how to use their God-given resources to become sustainable.

Additional Resources

BY GARY MILLER

Books

Kingdom-Focused Finances for the Family

This first book in the Kingdom-Focused Living series is realistic, humorous, and serious about getting us to become stewards instead of owners.

Charting a Course in Your Youth

A serious call to youth to examine their faith, focus, and finances. Second book in Kingdom-Focused Living series.

Going Till You're Gone

A plea for godly examples—for older men and women who will demonstrate a kingdom-focused vision all the way to the finish line. Third book in Kingdom-Focused Living series.

The Other Side of the Wall

Stresses Biblical principles that apply to all Christians who want to reflect God's heart in giving. Applying these principles has the potential to change lives—first our own, and then the people God calls us to share with. Fourth book in Kingdom-Focused Living series.

It's Not Your Business

How involved in business should followers of Jesus be? Did God intend the workplace to play a prominent role in building His kingdom? Explore the benefits and dangers in business. Fifth and final book in the Kingdom-Focused Living series.

Budgeting Made Simple

A budgeting workbook in a ring binder; complements *Kingdom-Focused Finances for the Family*.

What Happened to Our Money?

Ignorance of Biblical money management can set young people on a path of financial hardship that results in anxiety, marital discord, depression, and envy. This short book presents foundational truths on which young couples can build their financial lives.

Life in a Global Village

Would your worldview change if the world population were shrunk to a village of one hundred people and you lived in that village? Full-color book.

This Side of the Global Wall

Pictures and graphs in this full-color book portray the unprecedented opportunities Americans have today. What are we doing with the resources God has given us?

Small Business Handbook

A manual used in microfinance programs in developing countries. Includes devotionals and practical business teaching. Ideal for missions and churches.

Following Jesus in Everyday Life

A teaching manual ideal for mission settings. Each lesson addresses a Biblical principle and includes a story and discussion questions. Black and white illustrations.

A Good Soldier of Jesus Christ

A teaching manual like *Following Jesus in Everyday Life*, but targeting youth.

Know Before You Go

Every year, thousands of Americans travel to distant countries to help the needy. But could some of these short-term mission trips be doing more harm than good? This book encourages us to reexamine our goals and methods, and prepares people to effectively interact with other cultures in short-term missions.

Jesus Really Said That?

This book presents five teachings of Jesus that are often missed, ignored, or rejected. It tells the story of Jeremy and Alicia, a couple who thought they understood Christianity and knew what it meant to be a Christian . . . until they began to look at what Jesus actually said!

Audio Books

Kingdom-Focused Finances for the Family, Charting a Course in Your Youth, Going Till You're Gone, The Other Side of the Wall, It's Not Your Business, and *Life in a Global Village.*

Seminars

Kingdom-Focused Finances—Audio

This three-session seminar takes you beyond our culture's view of money and possessions, and challenges you to examine your heart by looking at your treasure. Three CDs.

Kingdom-Focused Finances—Audio and Visual

Follow along on the slides Gary uses in his seminars while you listen to the presentation. A good tool for group study or individual use. A computer is needed to view these three CDs.